I0799592

WonderWorks

Decodable Reader

Unit 2

Mc Graw Hill

Contents

Sam Can See 1
Consonant Ss

We See a Map 9
Consonant Pp

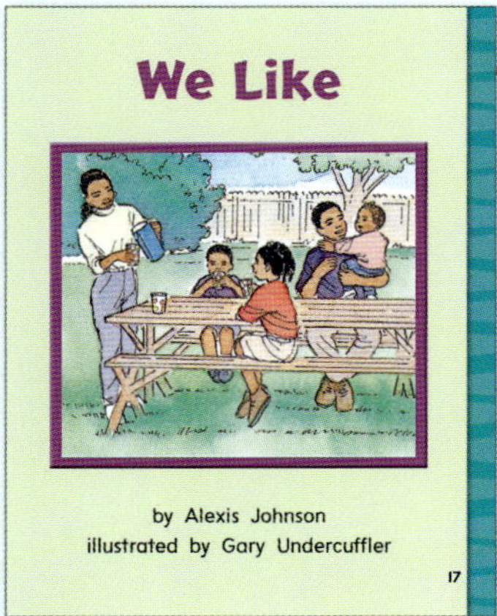

We Like........................ 17
Consonant Tt

Sam Can See

by Albert Miller
illustrated by Len Ebert

Sam can **see** the  .

tree

Sam can **see** the  .

bird

Sam can **see** the  .

leaves

Sam can **see** the 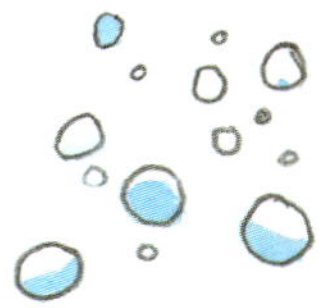 .

snow

Sam can **see** the  .

birds

Sam can **see** the  .

tree

We See a Map

by Malik Thomas

Johann Schumacher/Oxford Scientific/Getty Images

KEY TO MAP SYMBOLS
OGONNELLOE DISTRICT
Crossbill
Killanena
Flagmount
Slieve Aughty Mountains
Uggoon
Otter
Feakle
Hen Harrier
Scariff
Mountshannon
Holy Island
Lough Derg
Cloondoorney Lough
Tulla
R 352
Bodyke
Tuamgraney
Golf Course
Lough Bridget
Ogonnelloe
to Ennis
Magh Adair
Kilgory Lough
O'Callaghan's Mills
Pine Marten
Slieve Bernagh Mountains
Lough Cullaun
Doon Lough
Kilkishen
Cloniea Lough
Broadford
Kilbane
Craggaunowen Bronze Age Settlement
R 462
Knockshanvo
to Limerick
R 465
R 466
R 461
to Sixmilebridge
Major Trunk Road
Minor Regional Road
Wooded Areas

We see **a** map.

Andersen Ross/Blend Images/CORBIS

We see **a**  .

path

We see  .

trees

Johann Schumacher/Oxford Scientific/Getty Images

We see **a**  .

We see **a**  .

lake

Ed Reschke/Photolibrary/Getty Images

We see  .

flowers

We Like

by Alexis Johnson

illustrated by Gary Undercuffler

We **like** Pat.

We **like** Tam.

We **like**  .

Mom

We **like**  .

Dad

We **like** the  .

baby

We **like** the  .

family

Unit 2

Week 1 • *Sam Can See* .... page 1

Word Count: 27

Decodable Words

Target Phonics Element: Consonant /s/*s*

Sam

High-Frequency Words

see

Review: *can, the*

Week 2 • *We See a Map*...............page 9

Word Count: 22

Decodable Words

Target Phonics Element: Consonant /p/*p*

map

High-Frequency Words

a

Review: *can, see, we*

Week 3 • *We Like*......................... page 17

Word Count: 18

Decodable Words

Target Phonics Element: Consonant /t/*t*

Pat, Tam

High-Frequency Words

like

Review: *the, we*

Decoding skills taught to date:

Consonants /m/*m*, /s/*s*, /p/*p*, /t/*t*; Short *a*